Snowy Owls

SNOWY OWLS

Patricia Hunt

Illustrated with photographs

DODD, MEAD & COMPANY
New York

A SKYLIGHT BOOK

PHOTOGRAPH CREDITS

Gary R. Jones, 38, 59; Karl Maslowski, 8, 13, 31; Karl and Steve Maslowski, 43, 46; Steve Maslowski, 2, 18, 33, 55; David F. Parmelee, 16, 23, 26, 27, 40, 42, 49, 51, 52.

ACKNOWLEDGMENT

My special thanks to David F. Parmelee for supplying research material and photographs for this book.

1 2 3 4 5 6 7 8 9 10

Library of Congress Cataloging in Publication Data

Hunt, Patricia.
   Snowy owls.

   (A Skylight book)
   Includes index.
   Summary: Describes the physical characteristics, natural habitat, and life cycle of the snowy owl, a bird of prey of the far north.
     1. Snowy owl—Juvenile literature. [1. Snowy owl. 2. Owls] I. Title.
QL696.S83H86   598'.97   82-7361
ISBN 0-396-08073-1   AACR2

For Elizabeth and Bruno

Contents

Introduction   9

1   What Is a Snowy Owl?   11

2   Where the Snowy Owl Lives   20

3   The Snowies at Home   29

4   Courtship and Nesting   37

5   The Young Owlets   45

6   Enemies   54

7   The Past and the Future   57

Index   61

Snowy owls come into populated areas sometimes. Here one sits on a television antenna in Ohio.

Introduction

The winds of early winter swept across the salty Long Island marsh not far from the sea. The huge white owl sat quietly on an old fence post. It never moved. As wind gusts rippled its feathers every once in a while, the owl seemed to double in size. It looked like a huge mound of white feathers.

The white owl seemed to be sleeping. The eyes in its round head were closed down to tiny slits. After an hour or more, there was a tiny rustling sound in the grasses not far away. Instantly the owl's eyes became huge yellow circles. It drew its body more upright on its heavily feathered legs. It jerked its head around to the right to look intently in the direction of the sound.

9

Then the owl leaned forward a moment, raising the feathers from each side of its face. By doing this it uncovered two long ear slits so it could hear better. Quickly it pinpointed the spot where the sound came from. Opening up its wings, it lifted slightly into the air.

The owl glided over the grasses, hardly moving its wings and making no sound at all. After a few yards, it dove down into the grass with one foot thrust forward and all its claws fully extended.

It took only a second. Then the owl rose again into the air and returned to its perch—with a mouse in its mouth. Blinking its huge eyes and bobbing its head, it swallowed twice. The great snowy owl had caught itself a small but satisfying meal.

1

What Is a Snowy Owl?

The great snowy owl sometimes seems like a ghostly visitor from another world. Just what kind of bird is this impressive, powerful, and beautiful bird? Like hawks, falcons, and eagles, an owl is a bird of prey—a bird that captures living creatures for food.

The owl order, known as Strigiformes, can be found practically all over the world, from tropic forests to arctic lands. There are over 130 different kinds that range in size from only five inches to those that are two and a half feet tall. The snowy owl (*Nyctea scandiaca*) is among the largest, bigger even than the great horned owl of our own northern regions. The snowy stands 27 inches tall with a wingspread of 45 to more than 60 inches wide. When it takes off in flight, with its large wings fully spread apart, it is a breathtaking sight.

There is one major difference in the behavior of the snowies from most other owls. Owls almost always hunt and prowl at night. The snowy, however, is equally at home in both daytime and nighttime. The reason is that it is an arctic bird. In the arctic the summers have no nights; there is total daylight all the time. The winters have no sunlight; it is always dark. The snowy has adapted itself to sleep and to hunt in either full sunlight or total darkness.

Though the snowy is a large owl, it rarely looks fierce —but it can be. Sitting on a rock or post, it appears peaceful and almost cuddly, like a panda. But like a panda, looks are deceiving. Even if you had the opportunity, you never should try to pet a panda or tickle a snowy's feathery head.

A snowy owl appears to be so soft and harmless because its large curved beak and clawed feet are almost completely covered with feathers. The beak curves downward and is

Snowy owl

partially buried in feathers. The owl's legs and feet are covered in what look like high snow boots of feathers.

When the owl walks along the ground, its sharp talons or claws are withdrawn into its well-padded feet. When it perches on a rock or post, the talons are extended for a better grip. The snowy may grasp its perch with two toes forward and two back. Or with three toes forward and one back. Its outer front toe is very flexible and can move in any direction. It is as if your little finger could swivel around and point in either direction. This gives the owl a great advantage. It can use its foot like a hand when grabbing a mouse or other small animal.

The adult male snowy owl looks almost pure white, but when it flies, dark spots along its wings are noticeable. The female and young owls are streaked much more heavily with dark spots and bands of color. This is of benefit to the female as she nests on the ground. Her dark and white coloring makes her blend into the background of the earth, which at nesting time is often partially covered with snow.

The female snowy, in addition to differing in coloring from the male, is also larger than he is. This is often true

among other birds of prey. One possible reason for this is that the female broods the eggs and protects the young more actively than the male. Thus, she needs to be bigger and stronger.

Probably the most outstanding feature of snowy owls (and all owls) is their eyes. A snowy owl seems to be all eyes set in a bunch of feathers. The snowies' great round yellow eyes are like beacons in sun or darkness. The yellow iris of the eye expands and contracts, depending on the light and how sharply the owl wants to see. It is this ability to open up the iris that helps them to see in dim or dark light.

Unlike human eyes, an owl's eyes do not turn in their sockets to look sideways. Instead, the snowy must turn its head to see in different directions. To do this it has a very highly developed set of neck muscles. When it wants to look to the side, or behind, it turns its head. It cannot turn it completely around, but at times it almost seems to do so.

In addition to upper and lower eyelids, an owl's eye has a third eyelid called a nictitating membrane. This third eyelid serves as a protective covering for the eye. It is

Closeup of the snowy's golden eyes

milky in color and is pulled up from the bottom like the lower lid. This nictitating membrane clears its vision, much as eyedrops may do for us. But don't be fooled. If you should see what looks like a blind owl with whitish eyes, that owl can still see quite clearly right through those very special eyeshades.

Although the snowy owl doesn't appear to have any ears in its round head, it occasionally raises little tufts of feathers that look like ears or tiny horns. But they are just feathers. The ears are long slit-like openings that stretch from the top of the skull, behind its eyes, down either side of its face. Normally these slits are not visible, since they are completely covered with feathers. But when the snowy hears something rustling in the snow or grass, it raises its face feathers so as to catch the sound more clearly. It is only possible to see the ear slits when the owl is "listening."

All owls, including the snowy, are excellent flyers, and they seem to fly without making a sound. This is one reason they have a ghostly reputation. They appear silently and just as silently disappear. The big pheasants, the swans, ducks, and even smaller birds all make a wind noise when

they fly. Their wings whistle and whir, particularly as they take off. This is not true of owls. Owls have very long wings, far longer than would seem necessary to carry their light-boned bodies. This means that their weight is spread over a large surface when flying, making it unnecessary to keep flapping their wings so rapidly. Also, the long primary flight feathers of other birds, called pinions, are stiff. The owl's pinions are covered at the edge with a soft, velvet-like fringe. As a result, there is barely any sound as their wings beat through the air. The owl can rise, fall, glide, and fly with little effort. It is as buoyant in the air as a rubber ball in water. No wonder few of us ever hear the snowy if it drops in for a visit from the north. It is so silent it is easily overlooked.

A snowy owl flying in over the tundra

2

Where the Snowy Owl Lives

The permanent home of the snowy owl is the vast, barren northern country made up of parts of Canada, Europe, Russia, and Greenland—lands around the North Pole. This area, called the tundra, is bleak and cold and almost treeless, except at the far edges. It is covered with snow most of the winter. Only during a few months of full summer does the snow melt and the tundra earth appear. Just below the surface there is always a frozen mixture of soil, rocks, and water known as permafrost. This base of the tundra never melts. In summer, however, the top surface may be covered by a thin carpet of mosses and lichens. In some of the valleys, near river edges, there is grass. Here and there frost mounds pile up like icy eruptions. Sometimes they reach ten feet in height. Rock piles, too, can occur in various parts of the tundra. These higher places sometimes provide little landing fields and more often than not, they are the favorite perches of snowy owls.

In late spring the snow covering of the tundra melts, leaving the earth spongy and marshy. In some places small ponds develop. In the late spring, birds such as ducks and geese often migrate to these tundra ponds to raise their young. The area looks inviting for a few short weeks, with some small flowers coming into bloom. But it is not for long. These northern lands are mostly cold and bleak.

THE NEIGHBORS OF THE SNOWY

There are quite a few permanent residents of this area. The most numerous of all is the little lemming. A member of the rodent family, the lemming looks like a small hamster. It measures about five inches from the tip of its nose to the end of its stubby little tail. The lemming has a thick coat of fur over a fat body which helps keep it warm in this cold climate. In the deep winter, they curl up in moss or grass just below the snow. Lemmings make snow tunnels, which extend out in every direction so they can look for grass and other food under the snow. In spring when the snow starts melting, their tunnels become little underground streams, and the lemmings are flooded out of their winter hiding places. They pop up all over, looking bedraggled and water-soaked. As soon as their heads are visible, they must be on guard. The owls, and other predators, are just waiting to spot their brown bodies.

The relationship of the lemming and the owl is very important to the well-being of the owl. If it weren't for lemmings, owls might have a hard time finding enough to eat. Lemmings are their principal food, though they also catch a wide variety of other little animals and birds. But lemmings are not always plentiful. Their population keeps increasing and decreasing in cycles that run about four years. For instance, one year, there may not be many lemmings, so they are very timid and shy and stay in hiding. During that year their birthrate is quite low. The next year, their numbers increase a bit and their birthrate is larger.

A lemming at its burrow entrance

Now they start becoming bolder, coming out into the open more and more. By the third year they are even more numerous, and in the fourth year there are so many lemmings around that no owl could go hungry. In that fourth year a female lemming has five babies every 21 days. A lemming pair in this fourth year can produce some 16,000 descendants. Now the lemmings are in trouble, for there are so many of them they can't find enough vegetation to eat. They become nervous and fight with each other. They start running this way and that frantically looking for food. Finally they form into hungry armies and set out to search for food somewhere else. They start migrating to unknown places. Now the tundra is covered with lemmings and the owls, as well as other predators, have a feast. Because there is so much food available, the owls, too, now start raising large families. It is a time of plenty for them. But by the end of the fourth year all these frantic lemmings seem to be gone—eaten up, dead from starvation, drowning, or overactivity. The land appears empty once again and the lemmings, now, are very scarce. The cycle starts all over again. When this happens the owls that first year may not nest at all but wander the tundra seeking other food instead of raising a family.

There are other residents of the tundra. There is the ground squirrel, a plump, sandy-colored rodent with a long tail. It hibernates in deep sleep during the cold months in rocky crevices or along stream banks. It cannot make a true underground home as other ground squirrels do because it is unable to dig through the ice-hard permafrost. In spring it emerges from its long sleep and creeps about, feeding on leaves and insects, trying not to be caught by foxes, wolves, or snowy owls.

Arctic hares and snowshoe hares are also permanent residents that the owl hunts. The snowshoe hare has a winter coat of fur that changes to brown in summer to help camouflage it from all predators.

The wandering caribou is another animal that can be seen tramping across the tundra twice a year. Though it never stops for long, it seems to be constantly arriving and leaving as it heads for its breeding areas, summer grazing areas, or wintering spots. The long lines of caribou are usually watched over by wolves that move along with them

Arctic hares

trying to grab a meal. The owls are not bothered by the caribou armies. When the owls are nesting on the ground and might be in the way of the tramping feet, the caribou are far off in their breeding areas.

Another large bird that lives in the area all year round

A rock ptarmigan

and also nests on the ground is the ptarmigan—or grouse —of the Far North. It turns white in winter, but once the female ptarmigan lays her eggs, her feathers partially change to brown so that she blends into the scenery better. The male ptarmigan stays white all year, but helps pro-

27

tect the nest by decoying foxes and other predators away from the nest site.

During the brief summer of this area over 150 different kinds of birds from North America arrive to nest on the many streams and ponds.

3

The Snowies at Home

Snowy owls live by themselves in the tundra world for at least half the year, only pairing up in springtime to raise a family. Each bird, male or female, keeps a favorite perch or two where it will sit for hours and that, in a way, is its home most of the time.

However, when spring comes, the male stakes out a very definite amount of territory that is home. It is about a mile wide in an area that he is most familiar with and usually has several perches within its boundaries. The male booms out loud calls in the spring to mark his territorial area and to alert a female that he is at home and she should join him for the nesting season. Once a couple pairs together, this territory is their home during spring and summer. It is here that they will mate and raise their young. In late fall when the cold and snows return, the pair scatters in different directions to go back to their solitary ways.

How the Snowy Hunts

The snowy must hunt to eat—fresh meat or fish. The lemmings and other small ground-living creatures, such as voles, make up as much as 80 percent of its food.

The owl does its hunting largely by sitting and waiting. It will perch like a statue in one spot, apparently uninterested in what is going on about it. The only sign of movement may be its head that will turn first in one direction, then another. This may go on for hours. As it sits this way, the owl is often hunched down and appears to be resting, and sometimes it may be. But its ears are always on the alert and at the tiniest sound the owl opens its great eyes and stares in the direction of the sound. When the owl pinpoints the spot where it detects movement (even under the snow in winter), it jumps down on the ground. It hops

A snowy owl sits on a perch looking for prey.

about clumsily until, with a swift movement, it can thrust out its clawed foot and catch hold of the victim. Once in its grasp, the owl flies back to its perch, gulps and bobs its head up and down once or twice as it swallows its meal whole. If the creature is a ground squirrel, it may have to tear apart its meat first with its curved beak. Lemmings and voles go down whole.

Even when it is more actively on the prowl, the owl seems to do its hunting lazily. It will glide over the land, just a few yards up in the air, scanning this way and that. It hopes to scare a small creature out of hiding. When lemmings are plentiful and to be seen everywhere, this is an easy way to catch them.

Although the smaller animals are its main food supply, the owl will also hunt and capture many other kinds of creatures when the opportunity is there. Arctic hares are a part of its diet. They, like the lemmings, have cycles of high and low populations. When the owl spots a hare, it flies overhead. At first the hare may freeze in terror, then

A snowy owl carrying prey to its young.

nervously bang the ground with its hind feet. If able, it lopes for any nearby cover. The owl overtakes the hare, however, and with one fast swoop, grabs it on the ground with one foot while it uses the other foot as a brake in the snow or earth. If the hare is large and strong, the owl may open its wings halfway to help it brake to a full stop. The technique is somewhat the same as an airplane coming in for a landing, and reversing its jet engines to brake its forward speed.

The snowy also hunts small young birds to feed its young in the late spring and summer when the tundra ponds are filled with nesting ducks and geese. It may even hunt its year-round neighbor, the ptarmigan. This bird is much slower-moving than the owl. When the owl spots a ptarmigan on its nest or just sitting on the ground, it will fly overhead and dive-bomb the bird to try and spook it away from its nesting place. The ptarmigan will fly a short distance and then land on the ground. The owl follows and does the same—always coming closer and closer. It is a very precise hunting technique. The chase may go on for some time. The owl never seems to get tired but the heavy-

bodied ptarmigan does. Finally the owl moves in close and grabs its tired victim, usually on the ground. However, the owl is strong and skillful enough to be able to grab large birds in midair with its taloned feet.

In summer, when there are fish in the streams and ponds of the region, a hungry snowy owl may go fishing. It uses a very sly method. The famous early naturalist John James Audubon described how he once saw a snowy owl lie flat on a rock that bordered a small hole of water. He thought at first the bird was sleeping. Then apparently a fish swam by the rock, and the owl instantly reached out its foot and lifted the fish out of the water.

The reason the owl must resort to hunting everything it can is that it needs an enormous amount of food in a day. It is only well fed if it can eat enough food to equal its total body weight, which is about five pounds. It does not chew —merely bolts down its meal or pieces of its meal in a few gulps. The fur, feathers, beaks, toes, nails, and bones all disappear in those few gulps. But these parts are not digestible. As soon as it has eaten, the owl stretches and squeezes its stomach so as to mold all this "trash" into round pellets that it spits up after every meal. If an owl has a favorite spot where it rests most of the time, the area becomes covered with owl pellets.

4

Courtship and Nesting

Once spring comes, even though there may be snow on the ground, the male becomes very bold and loud. He spends much time soaring over the land checking out the food supply. If there are plenty of lemming and other game, the male goes courting in earnest. He will slowly wing through the air over his territory, then turn and drop toward the land before taking off again, hooting at the same time. He seems to be playing a game in the air, to attract a female to the area. When he spots a female, even as far away as a mile, he may quickly grab a lemming. Then with his gift in his claw, he lands and lays his prize within her sight. He may push it toward her, or he may lift his wings and walk round and round the lemming, hiding it

A male snowy owl bringing a lemming to a female.

from her view. Sometimes he stops and peers around his wing to see if she is watching. Then he may feel that one lemming is not enough, so he takes off again to bring her another.

When the female finally accepts his gifts, the pair go off flying together, gliding through the air, soaring upward and downward. The male may even dive, catch another lemming, fly back up in the sky and pass the lemming to the female with one foot while in midflight. This is an exciting time for the owls and unites the pair, but only for the breeding season. Next year the male will probably find another mate.

The female usually selects the nest site—perhaps a high spot near rocks, but more often right on the bare ground. The nest is very simple. She merely scratches out a round area that serves the purpose. She makes little or no attempt to furnish her nest. It is usually just a shallow hole in the ground.

The female snowy lays her eggs one at a time. After she drops the first pure white egg, she waits about four days before she lays another. This usually goes on until she has a total of eight to thirteen eggs under her. When she is alone on her nest guarding her brood of eggs, she is always on the lookout for predators—huge birds like the skua, or a creature like a fox or wolf. When threatened, she rises from her nest, spreads her wings, and barks. Then, if the predator comes nearer in spite of these efforts, she will

charge straight at it, her wings out, her feathers lifted so that she looks twice her size. When the male hears all the noisy commotion, he flies back to help. He lands and also charges, clattering his beak and barking even louder. Most predators back off from such determined and angry displays. But there is great danger for the eggs at this time, for as the parents are driving off a fox, a predatory bird can swoop down and grab an egg.

Besides being an active protector of his family, the male's main duty at this time is bringing back food for the female to eat. When the lemmings are plentiful, he piles them around the nest site in his eagerness to provide enough food, not only for his female but the owlets which begin hatching a month after the eggs are laid.

Since the eggs were not all laid at once, one egg at a time hatches. When the first tiny chick inside is ready to come out, it chips the egg covering with a tiny tooth on the upper part of its beak. As it tumbles out into the air, the owlet is blind, wet, and naked looking. Within a few hours,

A nest on the tundra

Snowy owl chicks and unhatched eggs

white down appears and covers its body like a little snow-
suit. In a few more hours it is hungry, and one of the parents has to stuff its mouth with small pieces of meat. Natu-
rally, at first, it cannot swallow a whole lemming or vole.
In three days' time, the first chick will have doubled its

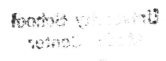

Male snowy owl feeding young

weight. By the fourth day, the next egg hatches, and in another four days the next, and so on.

When most of the eggs have hatched, the female will finally leave her nest briefly every once in a while to go hunting herself. As soon as she has fed herself, she returns to the nest with more meat and feeds any of the chicks that have hatched. She tears the meat into tiny pieces, grunts encouragingly as she pushes it down each throat in turn. Then she fluffs out her feathers, spreads her wings, pokes the few eggs that may still not have hatched under her and squats on them. If it snows, as it can in spring, or gets too warm, she sticks to her post, shielding the eggs. If she feels she cannot leave, she may mew a call to the male, reminding him to bring home some food. As soon as she sights him overhead, she bobs her head from side to side and grunts. As he lands, the two bow and grunt to each other and he presents the food he has caught. The couple, all through the nesting period, maintain these formal gestures to each other. It cements the affection between them.

5

The Young Owlets

By the time the nest is filled with a dozen or so baby owlets of different sizes, the nest home is getting over-crowded and dirty. The white feathery down that had covered the first chicks is replaced when they are ten days old by gray down and feathers. They do not look like snowy owls at all at this time. But these gray outfits are a protection, making them hard to see in the brownish-colored earth and mosses of the summer tundra. By the time the oldest chick is a month old, it becomes restless and totters out of the nest to do a little exploring. At first its thin legs are like rubber bands, and it staggers and shuffles like a little clown. But in a few hours, it becomes able to dash from this piece of cover to that. Even at this young

Female snowy owl with young in downy gray coats

age, the chick is instinctively timid and seemingly aware that there are dangers everywhere.

Soon the first chick is joined by some of the others, so that most of the brood is darting about like a bunch of schoolchildren at recess. However, they rarely go more than 100 yards from the nest, in any direction. Meanwhile, the male keeps returning with food and seems to keep track of all his chicks, for he brings food back for each of them. Just to be sure he doesn't overlook any of them, the little owlets squeal in piercing tones to attract his attention.

Finally, when all the chicks are fully clothed in the gray feather coats, the family leaves the nesting site and moves about the tundra searching for food. The young cannot fly as yet. It is not till they are two months old that they finally begin to try. They will jump in the air, flap their small wings, only to plop down on the ground. But they try over and over again. It takes a lot of practice for them to actually master the art of flying.

At about the same time a few white feathers begin to appear in their coats, giving them a gray and white checkerboard look. Their eyes are huge for their size. Their mouths are always opening up wide, hoping to be fed. But by this time they begin to learn how to catch their own food and, at last, to fly. Winter is coming and they must have attained their full size by then and be able to take care of themselves.

The parents show their young how to hunt and fly by their example. They also train them how to avoid predators if possible. In addition to putting on a fierce display, the parents also have a "broken-wing" act they use to decoy a predator away from the family group. To do this, one of the adult birds lifts its wings slightly, leans forward, and then suddenly goes limp as if in pain and ill. This arouses an approaching predator's interest—a fox perhaps. The fox thinks the owl will be an easy catch and zeroes in on the "sick" owl. But the snowy runs across the land, using one wing like a crutch, pretending the other wing is useless. It keeps moving away from the owl group, luring the fox as far afield as possible. Just as the fox seems to be getting near enough to pounce, the snowy takes off in angry, but triumphant, flight.

The young owlets rely not only on their parents for

Young nearly ready to fly—note "checkerboard" feathers

protection. While they cannot fly, they can sprint as fast as a runner for a short distance. They are also able to swim, using their wings as paddles. And, as a last resort, they instinctively will play "dead" like a possum if cornered, lying stiff and rigid on the ground, hoping the predator won't bother them.

By early autumn, the youngsters are about full grown and have turned adult white. They are now young juveniles ready to take care of themselves. Now the snowy owl family breaks up and each bird goes off on its own. If the food supply is plentiful, they may stay in one area, though usually a bit farther south than the breeding territories. But if there is little food, many of the owls migrate much farther south. The young juveniles are adventuresome and often end up in places like the marshes of Long Island, the open areas of the Middle Atlantic states, and the Far West. Some may even find their way as far south as Georgia and, in rare instances, the Caribbean. Snowies may turn up anywhere in winter, all alone or perhaps in a small group.

A young snowy owl "playing dead"

When a snowy owl reaches strange territory, it doesn't proclaim its presence by a lot of hooting. The owl that is far from its native home must compete with local predators, including other kinds of owls, for food. And man has never been a good friend of owls in the past. Farmers shoot snowies on sight when they see them, not realizing that the owls would help keep down the rodent population. Sometimes the owl just starves in strange places if it is unable to find enough food. But those that survive hunters and do find enough food return north in spring and head back to their favorite breeding area or set up a new one.

Snowy owl molting

6

Enemies

The most serious natural threat to the life of a snowy owl is starvation. In its northern haunts, an adult snowy has few enemies. A mob of small terns has been known to kill a hunting snowy. The small birds ganged up on the owl and before the owl realized what was happening, they were all over it, pecking it to death. This is rare, however.

The time the owl is most likely to be hunted and killed, of course, is when it is young. The owlets, from the time they are hatched, are easy prey for large roving birds like skuas, black-backed gulls, and other birds of prey like falcons. These birds can swoop down and grab a young owlet almost before the parents realize what is happening and put up a fight. Mammals like foxes, wolves, and even bears are

Polar bears are possible predators of the snowy owl.

also feared when the owlets are running about just learning to fly.

The final and real danger to snowies, as with so much wildlife, is man. Luckily, the circumpolar region of the world is not a place where man lives in any great numbers. The Indians and Eskimos of the area do rob snowy nests and kill the birds for food. Unfortunately sportsmen, too, sometimes seek out the bird to shoot as a trophy, largely because it is so beautiful. This, in the past, was quite a serious problem. Today, in most provinces of Canada and on the Shetland Islands off Scotland where snowies also breed, the owl is protected by law. But when the snowies migrate farther south in the winter looking for food, they are in almost constant danger from farmers and sportsmen.

7

The Past and the Future

From fossil remains, it is known that owls first appeared on earth some 50 million years ago. The snowy owl developed much later. It was around during the Paleolithic period about 15,000 years ago. In a cave in France a drawing was found some years ago of a snowy owl family made by early man that long ago. Since that was at a time when the Ice Age had brought the cold of the north down into Central Europe, it seems likely the snowy had migrated along with the cold. The early cave men of the time apparently admired the bird for its beauty but, no doubt, also hunted it for food.

Through later history, owls in general developed a bad reputation. They were thought to be evil spirits, creatures that flitted silently through the night. Because so many people were terrified of them, they called them omens of bad luck and death. Owls were also said to be companions of witches, who used them to cast their spells. On the other hand, there were people who decided this was not true, that, instead, owls were very wise birds. Athena, the Greek goddess of wisdom, was often shown with an owl on her shield. Merlin, the wise and magical friend of King Arthur, often appeared to the king with an owl on his shoulder that nibbled on his ear and told him wise things.

Since the snowy owl lives so far north, it has escaped being associated with all the evil and gloom. It was really only familiar to Indians and Eskimos. The Eskimos have many tales of its beauty and strength, and consider it a wise and clever bird. However, they still hunt it for food.

Now that we have learned more about the snowy owl and its way of life, we realize it is no wiser than any other bird, nor more evil. It has adapted well to its harsh environment and learned to survive under most difficult conditions. It deserves our admiration. It is hoped that it will never become endangered and instead remain a welcome visitor, not a creature to be hunted or hurt.

Index

Arctic hares, 25, 32, 34

Beak, 12, 14
Birds of prey, 11, 54
Black-backed gull, 54
"Broken-wing" act, 48

Caribou, 25–26
Claws, 10, 14
Climate, 12
Color, 14
Courtship, 37–39

Defense methods, 39, 41, 48, 50

Ears, 10, 17, 30
Eggs, 39, 41, 44
Enemies, 39, 41, 48, 53, 54, 56
Eskimos, 56, 58
Eyes, 15–16, 30, 47

Family group, 44, 47, 50
Feeding the young, 42, 44, 47

Feet, 12, 14, 32, 34, 35
Fish as food, 30, 35
Flight, 17, 19

Ground squirrels, 25
Growing up, 41–42, 45, 47–48, 50

Habitat, 20–21

Juveniles, 50

Kinds of owls, 11

Learning to fly, 47, 48
Legends, 57–58
Lemmings, 21–22, 24, 32, 37, 38, 39, 41, 42

Migration, 50
Moulting, 47, 50

Nest, 39, 41, 44, 45
Nictitating membrane, 15–16

Nyctea scandiaca (scientific name), 11

Owlets, 41–42, 44, 45, 47–48, 50

Pellets, 35–36
"Playing dead," 50
Ptarmigan, 26–27, 34–35

Scientific name. *See Nyctea scandiaca*
Size, 11, 14–15
Skua, 39, 54

Snowshoe hares, 25
Sounds, 29, 37, 41, 47

Talons. *See* Claws
Territory, 29–30
Toes, 14
Tundra, 20–21, 25

Voles, 30, 32, 42

Weight, 35
Wingspan, 11–12
Wolves, 25–26, 39, 54